Famiglia

Francis Dicandio

To order additional copies of this book, contact:
Xlibris
844-714-8691
www.Xlibris.com
Orders@Xlibris.com

ISBN: Softcover   979-8-3694-1169-8
        Hardcover   979-8-3694-1170-4
        EBook   979-8-3694-1168-1
Library of Congress Control Number: 2023922249
Print information available on the last page

Rev. date: 11/19/2023

Dedication!

'To my son
Jason Dicandio
always on my
mind'

I want to thank Nicole Caliendo for editing and
proofreading my manuscript, and Theresa Stella
for coming up with great ideas for my book!

Thank you

Inside Cover of Book!

Accomplishment!

1. Stress of mailing a letter
2. Heartache of a letter
3. Simple Italian cooking my way
4. Invasion from Mars to Earth
5. How am I supposed to say goodby
6. Family

GROWING UP ITALIAN

To begin, I have to go back where it all started - a region in Italy called Campania, Naples, where my grandmother, Rose Marietta, was born in 1887. My grandmother decided to flee Italy and come to the United States with the rise of the dictator, Bento Mussolini, who ruled from 1922 to 1943. The people of Italy were under his very strict and oppressive rule, so my grandmother and grandfather – Giovanni, born in 1888 – traveled thousands of miles to come to America, thinking that the streets were lined with gold. Boy, were they in for a big surprise! They came to America with six children, one boy and five girls. One of those girls was my mother, Dora, who was born in 1922 and died on May 23, 1994. God bless her soul. I love you, mom. I believe my mother was only five years old when she came to this country, and many thousands who followed her had to go through Ellis Island, located in the upper New York Bay area. The immigration station was established on January 1, 1882. Once immigrants came through Ellis Island, they had to go through a lengthy and laborious process to become a legal citizen. We'll talk about Ellis Island more in the coming pages.

My grandmother and grandfather headed to Brooklyn, New York and finally realized that the streets were not paved with gold after all. Now, don't ask me how my grandparents were able to come up with enough money to buy a two-family house in Williamsburg, Brooklyn on Grant Street, between Lorimer Street and Leonard Street! (I'm thinking that maybe my grandfather was mob connected - who knows?) The house had two stores - a pizzeria/bread store and a deli – attached to the house. Anyway, my grandparents lived on the first floor. Me and my two sisters - Angela and Roseann - and mom and dad lived on the second floor, and on top of all that we had a great big yard to play in. I have to say that me and my two sisters had great memories growing up in Brooklyn.

My dad was a veteran who got a job with the United States Postal Service after serving in World War II. My dad raised his family on $75 a week. My mom never worked a day in her life. My dad would say, "You have a full-time job raising three children and having food on the table when I get home from work at 5 o'clock." If my mom didn't have his food ready, all hell would break lose.

I was born on April 2, 1952. My parents sent me and my two sisters to Saint Mary's school, also called Immaculate Conception, which went up to the eighth grade. I was six years old in the first grade in 1958. I'm going to tell you some of the toys me and my sisters played with back in those days. We had the hula hoop, Mr. Potato Head, slinky, the great Frisbee, and Barbie Dolls were a big deal. The games we played included jump rope, hopscotch, tag, stoop ball, and one of my favorites – Scully, which was played with bottle caps.

I want to go back and talk about Catholic school. It was worse than the military. There were only 15 children to a classroom and we didn't have teachers like kids have today - we had monsters, and they were called nuns and they were completely covered from head to toe in black, and if you didn't stay in line you would get your ass kicked, as I did many times. One day in school, I got caught talking in class. The monster called me to her desk in front of the entire class and pulled out this long steel ruler that looked like a samurai sword. She told me to make a fist and then continued to whack my knuckles with that steel ruler 10 times on each hand - ouch! I was only 10 years old when this happened. Believe me, I wanted to kick her ass. Catholic school was a trip, but all in all I had good times and bad times.

The '50s and '60s were a lot different than growing up today. I mean, teachers and your parents can be in big trouble if they use their hands on you today. Times certainly have changed. There were many times I can remember being pulled by my hair from my desk, dragged into the hallway and smacked in my face. You tell this to people today and they will say you are crazy. The church was another big deal in Catholic school. The priest in the church was like a big dictator over a country; he controlled everything, and the priest always had the final word - no questions asked. Now, let's not forget that both my sisters went to the same school, but the girls were treated with a little more kindness than the boys. But when I became an altar boy, the nuns left me alone. Maybe they finally realized that I was friendly, or maybe they left me alone because I was working with the priest - who knows?

I want to talk about the year 1963. I was 13 years old in the seventh grade. I was sitting in the living room with my family watching TV when a special bulletin came on the air that John F. Kennedy was assassinated, shot in the head in Dallas Texas. That blew my mind. The 35th President of the United Stated died on November 22, 1963 at only 55 years old, shot by Lee Harvey Oswald.

Let's go back to growing up in Brooklyn. A slice of pizza back then was .15 cents, which is hard to believe. Subway fare was also .15 cents. A brand-new car was $3,000 – wow! And my favorite drink of all time was a chocolate egg cream and, no, it's not made with eggs or cream. It's made with only three ingredients - chocolate, milk, and seltzer, and a long spoon for stirring. The best chocolate to use to make an egg cream was U-Bet.

Now let's talk about some of the candy bars I grew up with back in the day, like Baby Ruth - named after the baseball player - Pay Day, Bit O' Honey, and the Chocolate cream bar, created by Joseph Fry 1866, the oldest candy bar in the world. Chunky, good and plenty. I could go on and on. After eight years of getting beaten by the monsters - I mean, nuns, I finally graduated at 14 years old in 1968. I decided to go to public high school called Eli Whitney, a vocational trade school on the north side of Brooklyn. I took all the trades electrical, electronics, cabinetmaking, plumbing, and upholstery. I like the idea of working with my hands so I took cabinetmaking and learned how to make furniture. This side of Brooklyn was a rough neighborhood. It was a mix of whites, Blacks and Puerto Ricans. Getting into fights after school was a normal thing, you had to learn how to handle yourself or you never survive. My brother-in-law John Zerga can relate to this. My sisters went to the same school and I had to look out for them. Back then, there were drugs all over the place, people shooting heroin into their veins. Heroin was the drug of choice in that time, young men and women were dying all over the place. I stayed far away from drugs. To be honest, my problem wasn't drugs, it was women. You could call me a womanizer. I wouldn't call myself a Don Juan, but let me put it this way, I had a few girlfriends back in the neighborhood. I picked up another bad habit, if you call it that, shooting pool, my favorite pastime back in the day. I would cut class every chance I could get and run to the pool, I played straight pool, eight ball, nine ball, a money game which I played most often. The first person to sink the nine balls in rotation wins the money, the players decide how much money they want to play. I grew up with no cell phone. We had what you call a rotary phone with letters and numbers. Now, let's say if you were outside, and you had to make a call, you would have to come home to make that call. And if someone called you while you were outside, if u didn't have a phone recorder you were out of luck. From 1926 to 1967. Television was entirely in black and white, and we had only 13 channels. Hard to believe today. I have to be truthful, knowing the technology we have today, I couldn't go back in time. The kids today don't realize how easy they have it. It seems to me like the new generations are getting weaker and weaker. I mean men want to be women, and women want to be men. What the hell is going on. And talking about this transgender bullshit, now I'm totally confused ...... I want to talk a little bit about my brother-in-law, John Zerga who lived in the same neighborhood. Okay, John, let's go down memory lane together. Manhattan Special. Was the big soda drink in our time and to this day I still drink it and love it. The Manhattan Special bottling company is located 340 Manhattan Ave, Brooklyn, NY 11211. John, let's not forget doo-wop and rock'n'roll, one year after I was born popular bands like the Flamingos and the Drifters, my favorite, emerged. Hey John, here comes your favorite group. Frankie Valli and the Four Seasons. Number one hit in 1960 was Sherry. Here is another one of your favorites .... UP ON THE ROOF by the Drifters, recorded in 1962. Now, back in the day, we would hang out on the corner of Ainslie Street and Manhattan Avenue, at Bennys candy store. Wow, where does the time go. What great times we had, hang out on the block, doo-wop sounds all around us. A song came out at the time called UP ON THE ROOF. Let me tell you why. My brother-in-law John was so thrilled about the song. John had a pigeon coop and spent a lot of time up there with my sister Angela. All our friends on the block, including myself, would wonder why he took Angela up on the roof. I'm sure there were no stars. Most likely my brother-in-law took her there because they will fully around. If you get my drift. Thank God, happily married over 50 years. DON'T LAUGH JOHN . I mean about being HAPPY. It's 3 o'clock in the morning and as I write this book, I have up on the roof in my head. I climbed way up to the top of those stairs, and all my cares drifted right into space. I wish that was true today.

I have to mention my first cousin on my mother's side, Nancy, who lived in Greenwich, Connecticut with all her rich friends and who had a silver spoon in her mouth. RIGHT, NAN? But even though she lived in Connecticut she loved coming to Brooklyn every summer to hang out with us on the block and see the boys. God, what great memories I have of hanging out on the block in the summertime in good old Brooklyn. I remember me and my two sisters coming home from school at 3 o'clock to play. God forbid if we came home past 5 o'clock when the big Gestapo – my father - came home and all hell would break lose. My poor mother was given an allowance by the Gestapo of $10, left on the stove every day when he left for work.

I'd like to talk about some of the movies back in the day. In 1955, *Godzilla,* one of my favorite movies of all time, as well as *Tarantula,* came out in the movies. In 1956 *Forbidden Planet* came out, as well as *The Mole People. The Incredible Shrinking Man* came out in 1957. In 1958, *The Blob* came out and starred Steve McQueen. What a great time in my life. Back then at the movies, you got to see a double feature, meaning you got to see two movies for the price of one - what a great deal!

I want to mention the baby boomers, born 1946 to 1964, ages 54 to 72 years old. As a kid, I had a shoe shine box and I would come home after school and get my shine box trying to hustle to make a buck. $.25 cents, $.50 cents for a shine. Today in the 21st century, people don't even wear shoes; sneakers are the big deal. Shoe shining is almost obsolete.

I have to mention Coney Island's famous Nathan's hot dogs. Nathan's was founded in 1916 by Nathan Handwerker and his wife Ida. It started over 100 years ago. Whenever I'm in the area I stop and down one or two dogs with mustard and sauerkraut, priced at about $4.75 each. I have to mention also that their French fries are the best.

I need to mention my first cousin on my mother's side is named Salvatore Bartoli, and he was born on October 29 and died on November 27, 2011. Sal was what I called him all my life. We had a very close relationship growing up in Brooklyn. He, along with my dad, his mom, and my aunt Tessie on my mom's side, worked for the United States Postal Service. Sal was also a Vietnam Vet who served in Da Nang Vietnam. I thank you for your service, and I think about you every day, Sal.

My aunt also had a husband, and his name was Emilio. I called him Uncle Emilio. I almost forgot that he also had a sister by the name of Susie. We were one HAPPY FAMILY. Well not, so fast. My aunt and uncle also had another son. His name was John (Giovanni in Italian). As I was told, at about the age of 11 or 12, he started getting severe pain in his tooth. I'm assuming it turned out to be some form of cancer. The poor boy was suffering and in excruciating pain. His suffering ended when he passed away. I'm sure my aunt and uncle's hearts fell to the ground. I could understand losing your parents, but I can't think of anything right now writing this book more devastating than losing a child. I know now that it affected my uncle more than I could ever imagine. From the day he lost his son, he was never the same. God bless you, Uncle Emilio. You are in a better place. I love you, uncle Emilio, and I love you, Aunt Tessie. You had such a hard life. Rest in peace.

Remember that this is all about growing up in Brooklyn from 1952, when I was born, to 1971, when I graduated high school. I want to go back and talk about the house my grandmother owned at 587 Grant St in Brooklyn. It's amazing how I still remember the address. On the corner of my block was Conti supermarket. The owner of that supermarket was a man by the name of Patsy. Don't ask me how I know, but Patsy was mob connected. After my grandmother passed away, Patsy was interested in buying my grandmother's building. Why did he want to buy my grandmother's building? Well, to build a parking lot for his customers, of course. At that time, my mother Dora was the owner of the building and she refused to sell to Patsy. That turned out to be a big mistake, so Patsy and the mob made us an offer we couldn't refuse. My family was afraid of what they might do – I'm assuming either burn the building down or come up with another solution to get rid of us. I will never forget the day that Patsy approached my father with a suitcase filled with money. It was somewhere I'm assuming between 20,000 thousand and 30,000 thousand dollars, and at that time, it was considered to be a lot of money. So, to make a long story short, we packed up our belongings and moved to 7411 Cypress Hill St. in Glendale, Queens and that's the end of that story.

From 1940 to 1973 men were drafted into the American army. The draft came to an end when the United States Armed Forces moved to an all-volunteer military force. But in 1971, the Vietnam war was still going strong, and a lottery was held for men born in 1952, which included me. The highest lottery number called for that group was 95. All men assigned that lottery number and the lower numbers were classified as available for military service and were called to report for induction. Guess what - my number was 23. What a graduation present! I was only 19 years old. My mother Dora was crying like a baby, and my father was in shock. SO NOW WHAT? My father didn't want to bury his son in Vietnam, I could understand that, so here is the scenario my father told me to consider: go to Kennedy Airport and get a one-way ticket to Canada. I said to my dad, "Are you crazy?" I would never be able to come back to the United States ever again. I told my father that this was war time, and I considered desertion committed in the time of war to be dishonorable. I told my dad that I had a better suggestion. I'd volunteer into a military service of my choice, and it wouldn't be the Army or the Marines. I told my dad that I wanted to join the United States Navy and that's just what I did. Both my parents drove me to Fort Hamilton. It was heartbreaking saying goodbye to both my parents, not knowing if I would ever see them again. I was sworn in and had to report to the Naval Station in Great Lakes, Chicago, Illinois. Boot camp training for 13 weeks in the winter time from November to January was very hard. It was freezing in Chicago and I froze my ass off. I came home on liberty to see my family. I then left my family and had to report to a Norfolk, Virginia naval station. I was assigned to a destroyer called the USS Harold J Ellison DD 864. After one year, I was assigned to another destroyer, the USS Farragut DLG 6. We made a six-month cruise around the continent of South America and stopped in countries such as Venezuela, Brazil, Argentina, Bolivia, Peru, Columbia, Chile, and then went through the Panama Canal – wow! It was just unbelievable. I had a great time and carry great memories after leaving the USS Farragut DLG 6. In 1973 I was assigned to another destroyer, the USS Powell DD 839 in Newport, Rhode Island, from 1971 to 1974. I served on three Navy destroyers in 1974 and was discharged from the Brooklyn Navy yard on Kent St. in Brooklyn, NY.

I wanted to talk a little about my favorite subject – food! My favorite restaurant is Randazzos Clam Bar at 2017 Emmons Avenue, Sheepshead Bay Brooklyn, NY 11235. If you love fish like I do, this is the place. They make the best spaghetti and white clam sauce in the world, and don't forget the extra garlic! The next favorite restaurant is Patricia's at 35 Broadway in Williamsburg, Brooklyn. This is the only restaurant I was able to find where they make spaghetti and crabs – wow! Mama Mia. Another one is Don Pepe, the mob restaurant at 135-58 Lefferts Boulevard in South Ozone Park - amazing food, excellent service, and the stuffed artichokes are out of this world. Another one is Belmonte's at 32 Withers Street in Brooklyn. Belmonte's claims to be the oldest Italian restaurant in New York City but who knows? Another great one is La Stella at 7519 5th Avenue in Brooklyn. On September 22, 1966 at a restaurant in Brooklyn bearing the same name, feds found 13 mobsters in the private room, including four bosses, devouring a meal. Whoops! They were caught with their pants down. There is no place except in Brooklyn where you could find the best Italian restaurants. Now, if you are ever in Brooklyn, you have to go to an Italian pastry shop called the Fortunato Brothers, located at 289 Manhattan Avenue. If you love tiramisu, Italian cheesecake, cream puffs, chocolate mousse, black forest, strawberry shortcake, and an ice cream called gelato, Fortunato's is the place to go. I'll tell you, talking about Fortunato Brothers makes me want to run down there and get me a cappuccino and few cream puffs – Mama mia!

I don't know how true it is, but one day I heard my mother saying that when I was a baby, to stop me from crying, she would put espresso in my bottle to put me to sleep. You would think that would keep me up all night – who the hell knows what she was thinking at the time. Amen. Love you, mom. I remember as a kid walking down Grand Street with my mother, holding her hand. In the summer time, we would stop for lemon ice and just walk through the neighborhood. My mother was gorgeous when she was young. I remember going down the block and wondering why all the cars were blowing their horns, and then I realized they were blowing their horns to get my mother's attention. I mean, my mother wasn't flirting, she was just a good-looking woman, God bless. Then together we would go food shopping for the Gestapo - my father - who came home at 5 o'clock and wanted the food on the table promptly. I loved spending time with my mother. I was what you would call a "mama's boy." I was always up my mother's ass. You have to remember that I had two sisters and I was the only boy so I got special treatment. I was much closer to my mother than my father. I could talk to my mother about anything – God forbid I should mention sex in front of my father; he would have had a heart attack. If I had a problem with anything, I would go to my mother first. She was the one who did my homework with me and cooked for me and bought me my clothes. One day, when she took a shower, she raised her arm and felt a lump. It turned out to be cancer. Me and my two sisters decided to put my mother in Sloan-Kettering Hospital. They treated her with chemotherapy, the chemo administered intravenously in her arm. I went with her a few times. All the time my mother was going through this, she always had a smile on her face. I had tears in my eyes, hoping to God that he wouldn't take her away. As time went on, my mother was getting worse. My father was in a panic, confused, and didn't know what to do. I felt his pain. The doctors decided to do a mastectomy and remove one of her breasts. But when my father went to see her in the hospital, my mother lifted her hospital gown to show my father, and he almost passed out. Not only did they take one breast, but they took both. The doctors told my father that it would spread to the other breast, but we were never consulted. My mother was completely flat chested when I went to see her in the hospital. I had to hold my tears. They told my mother she was cancer free, but that's what they tell everyone. A few years passed and the cancer came back. At this point, I was praying to God, begging Him not to take this good woman away from me. My mother was now fighting for her life. I was only in my early 40s when this all came about. The cancer spread through her entire body. Doctors at Sloan-Kettering Hospital had to do a spinal tap on my mother, and it was so painful my sisters and I couldn't bear to watch her suffer like that. The whole family was at her bed side in Sloan-Kettering Hospital. She was gasping for breath and finally, after all the suffering, she took her last breath and she was gone. She died on May 23, 1994. I go to the cemetery every Sunday to say hello. Like I said in my cook book dedicated to my mother, I will carry you in my heart until I see you again. Love you, mom.

After my mother passed away, my father was never the same. My two sisters noticed that he was hanging pictures of my mother with thumbtacks all over the place. My parents were married over 50 years and, as any one of us who has lost a loved one knows, it changes the way your heart feels. There is always an empty void. My father was a hard-working, honest man, who always provided for his family and was a great father to me and my two sisters. I would always play catch with him in the backyard after he came home from work. There's one thing I remember my father loving to do, and that was to burn wood in the backyard. I don't know, maybe he was a firebug - just kidding! I have to admit it was a great pastime for me to spend time with my father. In the summer time, we would go to our favorite place - Rockaway Beach. My father would make peppers and eggs on Italian bread - Mama mia, they tasted so good. On our way home, we would stop at Pizza City or - let's not forget - the great Bow Wow, which was famous for their hot dogs, and my dad would down two dogs, French fries and a Coca-Cola. Oh my God, do I miss those days! And I miss you, dad. You were always there to protect me and the family. God bless you for that. I will never forget the night when I had a nose bleed. I must've been about 12 or 13 years old. I was bleeding as if I was a water faucet. It was in the winter, I remember, because it was snowing outside, and it was freezing. I was in my pajamas at 2 o'clock in the morning and I couldn't stop the bleeding. There was blood all over the place - all over the sheets, all over the floor. Even when I was carried down the stairs, blood dripped everywhere. You picked me up from my bed that night and drove me to the hospital and saved my life. I thank you for that. I have tears in my eyes right now thinking about all the times you were there for me, dad. I always looked up to you. I remember when I went to New York City community college in Brooklyn not too far from where you worked on Cadman Plaza in Brooklyn. I would meet you for lunch - just you and I - and you would always say to me, "I'll never turn my back on you." Even now as a man of 67, I will never forget those words until the day I die. You know I come and talk to you in the cemetery every Sunday and talk about the good old days growing up in Brooklyn, I know when mom died you seemed like you were giving up on life. I could relate to that; during certain times in my life, I felt the same way. Sometimes in life shit just happens. Hey dad, I have to remind you that you are the only one in all of Italy who puts pepperoni in their sauce. I've been to a million Italian restaurants and asked for pasta with pepperoni sauce, and they look at me like I'm crazy. If you like a little spice in your sauce, it's a great dish. You don't have to sauté the pepperoni; you just slice it in circles of about ¼ inch thickness and drop it into the sauce. I've made it for my son Jason and he loves it.

At about this time, my father started losing a lot of weight, which was not a good sign. He was in his 80s and was never sick a day in his life, never in a hospital, but my father was a big crybaby when it came to seeing the doctor. He found blood in his urine and it turned out to be prostate cancer. At the time, we were told it was too late; the doctors said that the cancer spread outside the prostate and it was just a matter of time. On June 16, 2004, the father whom I loved with all my heart passed away in Wyckoff Heights Hospital, 10 years after my mother died. When my mother and father passed away, there were no more Sunday gatherings, no more sitting at the table with my family. Italians on

Sunday got together to *mangia* (meaning "to eat") pasta, meatballs and braciola. After the main course, there was espresso and Italian pastries, and you would sit at the table and eat until you passed out. Promise me when I die, I want my casket shaped like a cannoli. When my parents passed away, my family was finished.

Not too long ago, I was walking down Havemeyer Street in Brooklyn. I struck up a conversation with an 87-year-old Italian man. He had a short and stocky build with steel gray hair. He greeted me on the street when I said hello, as though I were an old friend. I asked him how do you feel about the neighborhood. He said, I don't like it one bit. These yuppies. They're like gypsies in the house. You are the landlord, if you're not there to watch what's going on, the whole entire army moves in." I thought they were all rich. They all come into this one-bedroom apartment and they all chip in it to pay $1800 a month. And all different kinds of shit was going on. It's clear that the old man doesn't like the fact that the newcomers are doubling and tripling up instead of renting an entire apartment. He says this is what's going on in Williamsburg, but the old man says it goes deeper. For all this time the church here has been ringing the bell on Sunday morning to tell the people to go to services. But this yuppie shit has no respect. They made the church stop ringing the bell so that they could sleep. Can you imagine that?

I need to talk about McCarran Park in Brooklyn at 776 Lorimer Street. During the summer time, my mother would take all three of us to the pool, which opened at 11 AM and closed at 3 PM. What a great time in my life! I have to say my mother took us all over the place. She loved spending time with her children, and I loved spending time with my mom. I want to go into a little history about McCarran Park. Opened in 1906 and originally named Greenpoint Park, the park was renamed McCarran Park in 1909 after State Sen. Patrick H McCarran, who became a democratic boss in Brooklyn. McCarran Park pool has a network of secret tunnels. The pool fell into despair and eventually closed in 1984, but it was restored and reopened again in 2012. The McCarran Park outdoor movie summer screen is hugely popular; it's a free outdoor film series held in the park. A giant screen is set up on the baseball fields and films are shown on Wednesday evenings. If you lived in

Brooklyn back in my time, it was all about Manhattan, but now it's all about Brooklyn. In my opinion, it's the place to live. Brooklyn right now is called the hottest borough.

Now let's not forget about White Castle in Brooklyn. My father loved White Castle hamburgers. White Castle is the oldest hamburger restaurant chain in the United States. The first White Castle restaurant opened in Wichita, Kansas in 1921. The first McDonald's didn't open until 1948 by comparison. White Castle's signature food item is the small burgers, which are called sliders. At the turn of the new century, White Castle has continued to grow with the expansion plan on opening 20 to 25 outlets each year. My father could down anywhere from 5 to 10 burgers. White Castle remains privately owned. White Castle's average price of a hamburger today is $0.53 – WOW, how can you go wrong? If I decide to go to White Castle, I could down at least five hamburgers and a shake. My father always loved his dogs and hamburgers. I always remember sitting on the porch in Glendale with my father, and my father could hear the music of the Miser Softee ice cream truck from blocks away. He would have a large chocolate cone with chocolate sprinkles. Does anyone who grew up in Brooklyn like I did remember the Domino sugar refinery? It was built in 1882 and was the largest sugar refinery in the world. In 1917, while producing sugar for the allies, an explosion destroyed part of the plant, killing several workers. A crowd of more than 15,000 people gathered to watch the plant burn. There was serious concern that the explosion was the work of German agents. And also I need to mention the building of the Williamsburg Bridge in 1903. Thousands of the lower Eastside residents were living in tenements across the river and wanted a better life in Williamsburg Brooklyn. The neighborhood of Williamsburg became a mix of Italians, Puerto Ricans and Germans, but today the Jewish community has taken over. The real estate belongs to the Jewish people; they have the money and the influence, believe it or not. I have to give to credit to Jewish people; they stick together and help one another in times of trouble.

I need to talk a little about East New York, which falls into a category of Brooklyn neighborhoods that can be quite dangerous. Others, in varying degrees, include

Brownsville, Bushwick, Bedford-Stuyvesant, and Coney Island. These areas that I mentioned can be extremely dangerous. East New York is the largest area and has the highest crime rate, followed closely by neighboring Brownsville. The statistical risk of being attacked in these neighborhoods is quite high. Some will be motivated by curiosity about what life looks like in these communities. Also, these areas are actually quite interesting in terms of buildings, stores, and life there in general. The vast majority of residents are honest, hard-working folks who will be friendly if approached, the way anyone should be approached. I offer a few tips when you are in these neighborhoods. Be alert at all times. Never stare at anyone, avoid deserted areas, be careful about giving money to panhandlers, never try to project an image of toughness, don't carry a lot of cash openly, always be respectful, avoid groups of people hanging out on the corner. I called these The Rules of Brooklyn. Women, as a rule, should exercise more caution and should not walk in these areas alone. Walking with a man is less likely to attract attention. Walking with a man and a big dog is even better. People who look like they could be a cop or working in the area, for example a teacher, social worker, delivery person, store employee, are at less risk.

In 1974, I was discharged from the United States Navy in Brooklyn at the Brooklyn Navy. The Brooklyn Navy was established in 1801. From the early 1810s through the 1960s, it was an active shipyard for the United States Navy, and was also known as the United States Naval Shipyard. The Brooklyn shipyard produced war ships for the United States Navy through the 1870s and steel ships after the American Civil War in the 1860s. The Brooklyn Navy Yard has been expanded several times, and at its peak, covered over 356 acres. The evidence of its 75,000 workers during World War II earned the yard nickname, The Can-Do Shipyard. The Navy yard was deactivated as a military installation in 1966 but continued to be used by private industries. The facility now houses an industrial and commercial complex run by the New York City government, both related to shipping repairs and maintenance and as office and manufacturing space for non-maritime industries. The Brooklyn Navy today includes dozens of structures, some of which date to the 19th century. The Brooklyn Naval Hospital, a medical complex on the east side of the Brooklyn Navy yard site, served as the yard hospital from 1838 until 1948. Dry dock 1, one of six dry docks at the yard, was completed in 1851 and is listed as a New York City designated landmark. Foremost structures include Admirals Row, a grouping of office residences at the west end of the yard, which was torn down in 2016 to accommodate new construction. Several buildings were built in the late 20th and early 21st centuries as part of the city run commercial and industrial complex. A commander's residence, also a national historic landmark, is located away from the main Navy yard site.

Let's talk about some of the celebrities that grew up in Brooklyn. This is proof that this part of New York became very popular. As a matter of fact, in the past decade, many famous actors, singers, and artists have bought studios in Brooklyn. Some of the celebrities who live in Brooklyn include Matt Damon, Sarah Jessica Parker, Spike Lee, Larry King, and Edie Falco. As matter of fact, Edie Falco, star of the *Sopranos* and *Nurse Jackie,* said she'd never left and felt Brooklyn was part of her heart and soul. I myself lived in Brooklyn all my life. At present time, writing this book, I've lived here for 67 years and loving it. I wouldn't want to live anywhere else, but that's just me. I remember my first wife, Joann, wanted to move out to Long Island. I hate Long Island with a passion, I told my wife that she would have to carry me out in a body bag to leave Brooklyn. She changed her mind quickly and we stayed in Brooklyn. There are two other places - New Jersey and Staten Island - no way in hell would I move there. It's all about Brooklyn.

Let's meet the Queen of Williamsburg, Brooklyn. If you happen to take a stroll through Williamsburg, you might have the honor of running into the neighborhood's Queen Leonora Russo. The 89-year-old has lived in the same rent-controlled apartment on N. 11th Street in Williamsburg for 66 years and has become a local icon, known for her extravagant wardrobe and fancy clothes.

Thousands of people will get together in Williamsburg for a festival full of food, dancing and live music. Unlike other Brooklyn events, the Lady of Mount Camel and San Paolino di Nola Feast is based in the tradition that got its start in Italy over 1,000 years ago, with its centerpiece being a four-ton 72-foot tower. A part of the neighborhood's nearly two-week feast, known as the Giglio, is carried through the streets by over 100 men. The Giglio feast has been held in Williamsburg every July since 1903, nearly two decades before the better-know Feast of San Genaro was celebrated in Little Italy. Never being a religious event, the Church of our Lady of Mount Carmel took over the feast during the 1950s and combined it with the event honoring our Lady of Mount Carmel. The Giglio feast is celebrated for 12 days in July and leads to the Our Lady of Mount Carmel feast on the 16th. The church identified outside volunteers to be *paranzas,* meaning "lifters," to carry the Giglio. As the Wall Street Journal reported, the neighborhood, which is rapidly losing organizers of Italian descent, launched a campaign to recruit strong lifters, going to Italian American organizations and nearby fitness centers. They don't have to be Italian; you can get a fireman or a cop who may be Irish or Polish and they're engaged with their faith. Even if the Italian population is dwelling in Williamsburg, those in the community who have moved away return for the feast, which offers carnival rides, games, and lots of Italian sausages and powdered zeppoles.

I spoke about it earlier, but I must say it again: there is nothing that says old school Brooklyn more than a classic egg cream, a nostalgic concoction that contains neither egg, no cream. Every neighborhood candy store and luncheonette once served this soda fountain treat made with milk, seltzer, and chocolate syrup - and not just any chocolate syrup. No respectable egg cream was made with anything other than a healthy dose of Brooklyn's own Foxes U-Bet chocolate syrup. Take a tall, chilled, straight sided, 8-ounce glass, spoon in an inch of whole milk, then tilt the glass and spray seltzer onto the bowl of the spoon to make a big foamy chocolate head. Stir, drink, enjoy. Herman Fox began making Foxes chocolate syrup in the basement of his Brownsville brownstone in 1900. 20 years later, after traveling to Texas in the hope of getting rich drilling oil, Herman returned home broke, but with the little man's expression -You bet - he renamed his product and never looked back. Today, H. Fox & Company is run by third and fourth generation members of the Fox family.

Okay, I want to talk about the secret behind why New York bagels in Brooklyn are so good. The New York Empire State Building, dirty water dogs, and hurried people with no fear of cursing one another out. They were created in New York and have been around since immigrants arrived at Ellis Island, homesick and hungry. The problem is it's a lot harder to get a decent bagel outside New York than it should be, considering mounting evidence against the myth that New York's water is responsible for its legendary bagels. I'll admit, I thought that it was the water, which comes from the Catskills in upstate New York, that makes New York bagels so good. But that myth has been busted. Water plays a much smaller role than people think. The two most critical steps for a good bagel are letting the bagels ferment and rise at a slightly cool temperature at least overnight and briefly boiling them before baking. I love my Brooklyn bagels, with cream cheese and jelly, butter, lox, peanut butter, whatever my heart desires. Brooklyn has it all, forget about Manhattan. It's Brooklyn all the way.

Growing up in Brooklyn, I have to talk about the Brooklyn Dodgers. They were an American baseball team that was active in the major leagues from 1884 until 1957, after which the team moved to Los Angeles. The team is noted for signing Jackie Robinson in 1947 as the first black player in the modern major leagues. On May 28, 1957. In 1955, the World Series matched the Brooklyn Dodgers against the New York Yankees, with the Dodgers winning the series and capturing their first championship in history. It would be the only series the Dodgers won while based in Brooklyn, as Major League Baseball's National League voted to allow Brooklyn to move to Los Angeles after the 1957 season. This was the fifth time in nine years that the Yankees and the Dodgers met in the World Series, the Brooklyn Dodgers won six in the Pittsfield World Series - 1955, 1959, 1963, 1965, 1981, 1988.

I want to talk about Ebbets Field baseball stadium in Brooklyn. One of the most important places in Brooklyn history was built in 1913, at 1720 Bedford Avenue. The field was at the intersection of Bedford Avenue and Sullivan Place. It was February 23, 1960, 2 ½ years after the Brooklyn Dodgers played their last game at Ebbets Field, and the big metal ball had been summoned so it could be sent crashing into the ballpark and begin reducing it to rubble, and that was the end of Ebbets Field in Brooklyn. Nothing in life lasts forever.

I want to talk about one of my mother's sisters, my aunt Sadie, who lived in Byram, Connecticut, and who has passed on, God bless her soul. I have great memories of her when I was a child, running and playing with my two first cousins, Nancy and Sandy, who passed from cancer at a very young age. I know that her parents were devastated. I hate to repeat myself. You can lose your parents, but I can't think of anything more horrific than losing a child. I really can't. Life is so cruel, so much suffering. So much death. But let me talk about the good times at my aunt Sadie's home in Byram, Connecticut. My uncle Tommy always had a glass of wine in his hand and he could eat macaroni every day of the week. We now call macaroni "pasta." You know what I really remember at my aunt Sadie's house? This long concrete table from one end of the garage to the other end. My aunt Sadie always had a lot of people to feed and a lot food on this long concrete table – Mama mia, as I'm writing this book, I can smell the food coming from the garage. I can't forget those big bowling ball sized meatballs. And then she would bring this big bowl of macaroni -or pasta, whatever you want to call it - and the Italian grated cheese! Everyone would sit at this concrete table and dig in and all your troubles at that moment would just disappear. Love you, Aunt Sadie, for all the great memories.

I want to talk about Lundy's restaurant. Lundy's was more than a restaurant. It was a Brooklyn institution, an integral part of the borough's history and of its founders hardly successful, yet strangely tragic life. William Irving Lundy began his career in 1907 with a clam shack on the dock at Sheepshead Bay. By 1934, he was the owner of virtually the entire waterfront in the old fishing village and the proprietor of F. W. I. Lundy brothers, the largest restaurant in New York City. More than 2,800 patrons dined at long tables with hundreds more lined up outside. Fresh lobster, clams and fish came directly to the restaurant's kitchen from the fishing boats. Just steps away at the Sheepshead Bay piers, native New Yorkers and tourists piled in for the clam chowder, corn on the cob, buttery biscuits, and huckleberry pie with ice. Born in 1895, Lundy was a son of a wholesale fish merchant with powerful political ties in Brooklyn. Just 23 years old when his father died, he became the head of the family and the driving entrepreneur. With his three younger brothers, he formed Lundy's Brothers Co., selling oysters and clams from a barge moored in the bay and acquiring property all along the waterfront. But tragedy struck on a cold February day in 1920. His brother was attending the clam beds. A Jamaica Bay ice floe capsized the boat. Two of the brothers drowned in the icy waters. Shaken by the loss, he brought his three sisters into the business and, along with their surviving brother, opened his first restaurant. Lundy's became a recluse in an apartment over the restaurant. He continued to direct its operations leaving his apartment only to walk his 14 pet dogs at dawn. In the early 1970s, the restaurant came under siege of robberies, including several brutal attacks on the managers. The police suspected a connection to the Mafia, which controlled many businesses in Sheepshead Bay. Lundy refused to talk to the police, even after his youngest sister and brother-in-law were murdered. In 1977, Lundy was found dead in his apartment under suspicious circumstances. His death and the two murders remain a mystery.

I have to talk about my mother's other sister, my Aunt Mary. I have such great memories of her. What a great person she was, and smart. She had three children - Nancy, John, and Frankie - and a husband, my godfather, Uncle Frank. He was very generous with me every time he would see me; he would put a $10 bill in the palm of my hand, and at that time, I was young and $10 to me was a lot of money. He was a hard-working man like my dad. I would spend the summers up there to make a few bucks cutting the grass and doing whatever my uncle told me to do. It was good to get away from city life. They lived in Greenwich, Connecticut, with all the rich people. My Uncle Frank worked for the Jeffersons, who were multimillionaires. Aunt Mary was a homebody and a great cook. I know my Aunt Mary and my mother Dora are in heaven having an espresso together. You will always have a special place in my heart, God bless your soul. I would like to know where all these people disappear to. It's one of the mysteries of life. I guess we won't know until it happens to us.

You remember that old cliché. You are not getting older, you are getting better. It's a hopeful phrase but unrealistic. The first part is a simple lie, the second part is a possibility. Like it or not, we are getting older and, like it or not, nothing can be done about it. Even if we sincerely deny it, we are all getting older, and there is no use in exploring ways of stopping the process. Our bodies may indeed be wearing out as we grow old, but we can increase in wisdom. Being realistic is the key. I am now in my sixth decade as I write this book. I am 67 years old and getting older and my body and appearance are much different now when I look into the mirror. No more muscle mass hunching over, and I could go on and on about losing my sight, but, what can I do but take one day at a time? It's reasonable to assume that three thirds or more of my life on the earth are over, and my time under the earth is fast approaching. It's just reality. There is no use dreaming impossible dreams about the rest of my life on earth. My chances of finally becoming a basketball star are over and done with. I no longer have the time to become a brain surgeon. If the truth must be told, now that I come to age, I sense more freedom than I ever had before. I no longer feel driven to succeed. I have pretty much done what I am capable of doing. What a shame, at such a point in life, to have to suffer the pains of growing old. Just when I seem ready to use all my powers most effectively, they begin to fail. Who can make sense of that? Are we not more brittle than if we were made of glass? Yet even though glass is brittle, it lasts a long time. But we humans, brittle as we are, are also subjected to accidents in our lives and we cannot survive for a very long time. Sometimes when we get older, we mourn the loss of all past, saying, *Oh, if I could only experience again the innocent days of my childhood. If I could only experience again the passionate love given and received in my youth. If I can only experience again the feeling of accomplishment and success of my mid-years.* But now that I am old. Those days are lost forever. I can no longer look at life with simple wonder, believing that the unknown before me will be just fine. I can no longer look forward to being the *be all and end all* of someone else's love, nor can I dare to give my love in such a passionate way. I can no longer speak to the world from the mountain of my accomplishment and success. No one is interested in what I say as I slide down the evening side of my life towards the grave. Amen. Enough about getting old.

Let's talk about something sweet like Eddie's Sweet Shop, the oldest ice cream parlor in New York City. Like Katz's Deli, Delmonico's, and Lombardi's, Eddie's Sweet Shop on Metropolitan Avenue in Forest Hills is one of New York City's oldest eateries. Eddie's has been scooping homemade ice cream and toppings from behind the same marble countertops since around 1925. After the original Jahns franchise locations closed, Eddie's unofficially became the oldest ice cream shop in New York City, the owner, Vito Citrano says, "We just keep doing what we're doing day by day and don't think about it we don't change much, so you always know what you're going to get. When we bought the shop in 1968, it was already nostalgic." The Citrano family and their team of scoopers made all 18 flavors of ice cream from scratch, using the same recipes that Giuseppe, Vito's father, inherited from the shop's previous owners. The menu doesn't list any trendy ice cream flavors so don't even think about asking. The owner makes the whipped cream and all of their sauces by hand every day, including hot fudge and caramel. If you're not afraid of corn syrup, this place is not for you. The classic ice cream shop was particularly known for its towering classic sundaes with the works – hot fudge, homemade whipped cream and a cherry. While chocolate is one of the most popular selections, you can also order flavors like vanilla chip, coffee, maple, walnut, vanilla, and vanilla fudge. The owner also claims that Eddie's has a secret menu, but he would not say anything further about it. How is it a secret menu if everyone knows about it?

I am a Knights of Columbus member, and I'd like to talk about the organization. The order of the Knights of Columbus is the world's largest Catholic fraternity service organization. Founded in the United States in 1882, it has the name and the honor of Christopher Columbus and is dedicated to the principles of charity, unity and patriotism. Michael J. McGivney, an Irish American Catholic priest, founded the Knights of Columbus in New Haven, Connecticut. He gathered a group of men from St. Mary's Parish for an organizational meeting on October 2, 1881. A courageous journey of discovery, unfair attacks on Christopher Columbus, past and present, should not be allowed to obscure the truth about the man, his voyage and his motives. Born in Genoa, Italy, Columbus was a deeply Catholic Explorer who was willing to go against the grain. He believed he could reach the shores of Asia by sailing a mere 3,000 miles west across the Atlantic Ocean. Such a passage would establish faster and easier trade routes than were possible through overland travel or by sailing south and east around Africa. Scholars of this date calculated the distance to cross the Atlantic Ocean was over 7,000 miles, out of practical range for ships of the day. After 10 weeks, Columbus did indeed find land - not the outskirts of the Orient, as he went to his grave believing, but discovering an entirely new continent. And here we have it, the United States of America. Thank you, Christopher Columbus. Another great discovery by a great Italian explorer. Brooklyn, where Italian values, culture, and dreams thrive.

The first significant influx of Italian immigrants came during the 1800s. The 1855 New York Census did not list any Italian natives in Brooklyn. However, by 1890, there were 9,563 Italians residing in the borough. By 1900, Brooklyn's Italian population was second only to Manhattan. Although the last notable wave of Italian immigration ended in the 1960s, Italians remains one of the six prevailing foreign languages in New York.

The American dream was not easy for Italian Americans. They accepted jobs on the lowest rung of the occupational ladder, bypassing education in place of on-the-job training. From very humble beginnings, entrenched with determination, they rose to the top of American industry. Proud and thankful for their heritage, they made great strides for future generations. Men like Antonio Saltillo opened a bakery. Raised in South Brooklyn during World War II, when sugar was rationed, he began baking and selling bread in his pastry shop at 600 Fifth Avenue. *Everyone needs bread* became his slogan. He was right. He subsequently purchased real estate and established family businesses. Frustration and hard times and low wages did not discourage the spirit of the Italian people. When they had no church of their own, they built them. As the population of Italians grew, so did memberships of Italian nonprofit organizations such as the order Sons of Italy in America. An Italian proverb states, *He who leaves, succeeds.* But it took a lot of courage for immigrants to leave their villages where they were born, to say goodbye to the families, the sources of love and security, and set out for a land that was nothing more than a legend to many peasants of the South. More than 95% of all Italian immigrants followed the wake of Giovanni da Verrazano and arrived in New York City. They passed through the narrows between Brooklyn and Staten Island, where the bridge named in Verrazano's honor stands. From 1880 to 1930, New York City was one of the fastest growing urban areas in the world. Italians helped construct skyscrapers, bridges, tunnels, subways and streets. When the Brooklyn Bridge was built in 1883, in part by Italian laborers, Italian used it to move into the neighborhoods across the East River in Brooklyn, and that was just the beginning. Francis DiCandio loves his Italian culture. Italian culture is steeped in the arts, family, architecture, and music of Brooklyn.

Let's talk about Italy. About 93% of the Italian population speaks Italian as their native language. Italy is home to more than 62 million individuals as of 2017 and is ranked 23rd in population size when compared with other countries throughout the world. About 96% of the population of Italy is Italian, though there are many other ethnicities that live in this country. Family is an extremely important value in the Italian culture. Italians have frequent family gatherings and enjoy spending time with those in their family. Children are reared to remain close to the family. Football is a popular spectator and participation sport. The Italian national team is among the very best in the world. It has won the World Cup on four different occasions – 1934, 1938, 1982, and 2006. Only Brazil has a better record. Cycling is also a well-represented sport in Italy. Italian volleyball is another big sport in Italy. And believe it or not fencing is a very successful sport in Italy. It is one of the most successful fencing countries. One of the most remarkable wrestlers was Bruno Sammartino, who held the record of the WWWF world heavyweight championship for over 11 years. Another very popular sport in Italy is boxing.

I just want to say it's 10:30 at night and I'm drinking an espresso and eating a biscotti, which is an Italian word for cookie. Writing a book is not as easy as people think it is.

Some nights I'm completely blank and other nights I can't stop writing. I can't believe it. At my age of 67 years old, I found a hobby – writing, which keeps my mind occupied and keeps me out trouble.

There is one person that I think about all the time and that is my grandmother, Rose. I would love to talk to her today about when she was little and the hard times they had coming to this country. She was a walking history book. It's amazing when people are alive how we take them all for granted.

When one grows up Italian, they learn quickly that the most important things in life are celebrated with family. All events, birthdays, anniversaries, mothers and Father's Day, and even Sundays are reasons to gather, eat a lot and catch up on family business. They grow up believing America is the greatest country in the world, but at the same time, they are intensely proud to be the children, grandchildren, and grandchildren of immigrants. That heritage makes them the men and women that they are today. As a child, Italians see this is perfectly normal until, as an adult, they learn what drastically different ideas non-Italians may have about dinner or family in general. With Italians there is no distinction between the nuclear family and the rest of the family. Growing up, immersed in the culture and traditions of their ancestors' homeland, they heard the stories of the old country, and for some, it meant carrying on traditions. Men like Raymond and Philip Leone, proprietors of the Leone funeral home in Greenwood Heights, carried on the traditions of their parents, Anthony and Josephine, Italian immigrants who began the business in 1983. The same year, in Bensonhurst, the Geraldi family opened Tasty Bagels, where Vincent, Joe, and Angel are always on the premises., What I'm trying to point out as an Italian myself is that the children always follow their parents in whatever business they pursue. If your father was a shoemaker, you follow his footsteps. If your father was in the construction business, you are right behind him. Now, if your father was a gangster, well, that's a whole different story. It seems to me like the old Italian traditions are gone forever. It's really a shame and the younger generation have no idea what the hell is going on. They don't even know who their aunts and uncles are. It's just unbelievable. They have no family values and no respect for the Italian culture and are not even interested in learning about their heritage. When the older generation like myself is gone, forget about it.

Let me mention growing up Italian also meant going to mass every Sunday and holy days of Easter Sunday, Good Friday and Christmas. Sunday mass is a big part of the Italian family. I don't want to get into a big religious thing here but whether we realize it or not, many of the battles we face in our lives today are spiritual battles, and we cannot win with just our own willpower. When trouble comes your way, or when bad news hits you right between the eyes, be determined to replace fear with confidence in God, to replace worry with faith in Him, and to replace anxiety with His peace. Keep calm and most of all trust in God. Talking about anxiety, worry, fear, depression, pressure, regret, stress, frustration, self-criticism, seeking the approval of others, fear of the future, unexpected setbacks, we all need help with these problems. There is an old Indian saying: *All the worry in the world will not change what will happen tomorrow.* Remember those words.

Growing up Italian in Brooklyn with my parents, I have to talk about the music. My father, God bless his soul, thought he was an opera singer. My mother, God bless her soul, loved Ol' Blue Eyes Frank Sinatra, her favorite. My favorite was Dean Martin. I loved this voice. He made a few movies in his time and was a great personality, though he was a little heavy on the booze. His TV show was great.

For about a month, I had what they call writer's block. It's where you can't think of anything to write, but now I'm back on the scene, I have a little story I want to share with you. It's called ITALIAN MOM. A young Italian man excitedly tells his mother he's fallen in love and that he is going to get married. He says, "Just for you, ma, I'm going to bring over three women and you try to guess which one I'm going to marry." His mother agrees. The next day, he brings three beautiful women into the house and sits them down on the couch and chats for a while. He then says, "Okay, ma, guess which one I'm going to marry," and she immediately replies, "the one on the right."

"That's amazing Ma. You're right, how did you know that?"

The Italian mother replies, "I don't like her."

End of story.

You know growing up Italian in Brooklyn, I would spend many hours with my grandmother, Rose, in the backyard. My grandmother loved to plant and play around with the plants and get dirty. We spent many hours in the garden planting basil, tomatoes, zucchini, and many other vegetables. My grandma was also a great cook. I named my first cookbook, *Simple Italian Cooking My Way* because that's how my grandma would cook - simple.

For some reason, Italians love their fig trees. I know that every Italian who has a backyard has a fig tree. Most of us remember our grandparents wonderfully kept a backyard garden. In every backyard, there was, and still is, the always present fig tree, whether it be the common ground turkey, fig, or the Italian everbearing fig tree. Having a fig tree just seems to be the natural scheme of things. I was always told it was good luck for the family to have one growing in the yard and producing figs. My grandma said she was sitting under the family fig tree when my grandpa asked her to marry him, and soon after she was sitting on the same tree when she told her young husband that they were expecting their first child. The fig tree has been around since the earliest recorded history. Its fruit has been a staple for the richest and poorest of populations. The tree itself has always been a symbol of abundance, fertility and sweetness. The fruit of the fig tree are the seeds within inverted flowers. The fig tree typically grows between 10 to 30 feet tall, but can grow as tall as 50 feet. There abundance of leaves and fruit make them great shade trees as little sun passes through their branches. They need plenty of room around them, due to their size and their root system will travel beyond the reach of the branches. As of 2010, a wild fig tree in South Africa holds the record for the deepest tree roots, amongst all trees with roots reaching down 400 feet.

Growing up in an Italian family, you would smell basil all over the place, even down the block. The smell is just unbelievable. There is no Italian in this world that would cook without using basil of some kind. I'm going to give you a little history lesson about basil. The leaves of this plant are so delightful and habit-forming, you have to marvel that it hasn't been made illegal. Basil is undoubtedly the most loved popular herb in Italy. Although we tend to associate it with Italy and other Mediterranean countries, it actually originated in India and was brought to the Mediterranean via the spice roots in ancient times. If you're growing basil in your backyard or at a window, cut the basil leaves as needed for the kitchen from the top. The leaves grow back quickly. Basil preserves well so it can also be frozen. It is rich in antioxidants, and some claim it has anti-cancer and anti-viral properties. In Italy, basil is believed to help along the *penichella,* the after-lunch nap that millions of Italians still enjoy on hot summer afternoons. Mama mia, I love being Italian.

I need 200 pages to publish this book. So far, I only have only 45 pages. I have a long way to go, but I'll get through it. It is now the month of April. I get very depressed around this time. Born in 1952, I just turned 68 years old. Mama mia, where does the time go? Okay, now that my birthday past and I'm not depressed, I could enjoy the week before Easter Sunday, which is April 12th this year.

For Italians, Easter is a big deal. Everyone goes to mass and then they come home and stuff their faces with Sunday gravy, sausage, meatballs, braciola and lasagna. And then after our bellies are full, out comes the espresso and the St. Joseph's pastry. And then after all that food, my mother breaks out the bingo game. I miss those times when my mother and father were alive. Everyone went their separate ways and it was never the same for me. God bless them, wherever they are. So, Easter is over. Time marches on.

I have to mention something, but it has nothing to do with being Italian. It is April 12, 2020. New York City and the world have been hit with this coronavirus, which originated in China. Trump calls it the Chinese virus. Total deaths in Italy are over 21,000 people - unbelievable. In less than one month, Italy has gone from having only three cases of the coronavirus to having the highest number of cases and deaths throughout all 20 regions of the country. The number of cases rose by 50% on March 8th alone. The pandemic began in February, when a 38-year-old man checked himself into a local hospital in the town of Codogno in Lombardy. He tested positive for the virus, becoming the first recorded patient with COVID. The average age of coronavirus patients in Italy who have died because of the virus is 81 years old, according to the National Health Institute. Italy is the oldest country in the oldest continent in the world. We have a lot of people over the age of 65. The Italian government has taken the biggest steps outside of China to curb the spread of the disease. All public events are banned and schools have been canceled throughout the country. Public spaces, such as gyms, theaters and cinemas have also been closed by the government. Individuals who defy the lockdown could face up to three months in jail or a fine of $234, Mama mia, I can't believe my country is being destroyed by this virus that came from China. In my opinion, the government of China should pay the price, like many other countries that we help. In my opinion, the United States should take care of the United States and not worry about all these countries that hate us. This coronavirus from China should teach us a lesson - all of our medications, including antibiotics, should be made in the United States and stop illegal immigration from bringing all these diseases into this country. Build that wall and stop them from coming into this country. Otherwise, we are all going to die. The Chinese people eat bats, cats, dogs, snakes, rats - this is where the diseases are coming from. Putting cats and dogs in cages and chopping them up alive and burning them alive. Okay enough about the virus.

Let's get back to growing up Italian. A lot of my Italian friends say, *"Goomba,* how are you doing today?" Not everyone is a *goomba.* Alright, so now you asking yourself if you're a *goomba.* If you have to ask, the answer is probably no. But here are some ways to tell. A *goomba* will never back down from a fight, even if he is outnumbered or outmatched and he's about to get his ass kicked. A *goomba* will always stay in the fight until he can't fight any more. It's victory or the hospital. There is no in-between. A *goomba* will never let anyone insult his wife, his mother, or any other woman present. He's that kind of a gentleman. A *goomba* is usually a big guy. He's wearing a jogging suit, a pinky ring, a gold watch and gold chains. You're a *goomba* if your godfather is a godfather, your wife and your girlfriend are cousins, use the term *fat bastard* to show affection, your mother taught you how to shave, and every guy at your wedding is called Tony. This is just a few examples.

I have to mention something about Italians going to a funeral. There's always one person at every funeral who gets hysterical and starts screaming and then tries to climb into the coffin. I don't know what it is about Italians, but this always happens. At some point in the service, someone starts screaming. *No, no. Take me, I wanted to die. Bring him back. Take me instead!* And into the box they go. At an Italian's funeral, everyone is very emotional. Everyone starts crying. Women, girls, old men, young men, big men, and little men. Nothing to be ashamed about. After the funeral, everyone is starving and looking to go to an Italian restaurant. All the tears at the funeral fall away and food brings a smile to everyone's face. They already forgot who was lying in that coffin a few hours ago after stuffing their face. Everyone goes on their merry way and life goes on.

Let's talk a little about the Italian wedding. The wedding will start in the afternoon at the church, and it will go until almost the next morning. If you're the father of the bride, it's a point of honor to have the best wedding possible for your daughter. No expenses are spared. Here comes the weird part. Unlike weddings in other cultures, money actually changes hands at an Italian wedding. No one brings a toaster to Italian weddings. No Italian bride is registered at Macy's at a true Italian wedding. It's all cash. The family has spent a small fortune putting the wedding on, and the guests better come up with cash, too. In Italian, the money is called a boost. Everyone brings the boost. If the guest doesn't come up with the boost, or money, the guns are going to come out. Mark my words.

I want to talk about an incident in Howard Beach. In the 1980s, several racially motivated attacks dominated the headlines of New York City newspapers. On September 15, 1983, artist and model Michael Stewart died on the lower Manhattan subway platform from a chokehold and beating he received from several police officers. A year later, on October 29th, an elderly grandmother, Eleanor Bumpers, was murdered by a police officer in her Bronx apartment as he and other offices tried to evict her. Later that year, on December 22nd, a mam shot and seriously wounded four black teenagers whom he thought were going to rob him on the subway train in Manhattan. The Howard Beach racial incident in late 1986 propelled the predominantly Italian and Jewish communities into the national spotlight, exposing racial hatred in New York City. On the morning of December 5 20, 1986, a white mob attacked three stranded African-Americans in Howard Beach, a predominately white Italian community in the borough of Queens. On that night, four African-American men, Cedric Sandiford, 36, Timothy Grimes, 20, Michael Griffith, 23, and Curtis Sylvester, 20, were traveling in a 1976 Buick from their Brooklyn neighborhood to Queens to collect Griffith's paycheck. When the Buick stalled on Cross Bay Boulevard, near Howard Beach, Griffith, Sandiford and Grimes walked to Howard Beach to locate a pay phone. The three entered Howard Beach at midnight and were immediately confronted by a small group of white pedestrians, who yelled racial slurs and told them to get out of the neighborhood. However, by then hungry and tired, the men decided to dine and rest at the New Park pizzeria on Cross Bay Boulevard. When Sandiford, Grimes, and Griffith left the restaurant at 12:40 AM, 12 white youths awaited them with baseball bats, tire irons, and tree limbs. The gang, led by Jon Lester, 17, included Salvatore Desimone, 19, William Bollander, 17, James Povinelli, 16, Michael Pirone, 17, John Saggese, 19, Jason Ladone, 16, Thomas Gucciardo, 17, Harry Bunocore, 18, Scott Kern, 18, Thomas Farino, 16, and Robert Riley, 19. The mob attacked Griffith and Sandiford. Grimes, who drew a knife on the angry mob, escaped with minor injuries. Sandiford begged for his life before Lester knocked him down with a baseball bat. With the mob in hot pursuit, severely beaten Griffin ran to the nearby Belt Parkway, where he jumped through a small hole in a fence adjacent to the highway and staggered across a busy 6 lane expressway, trying to escape his attackers. He was hit and instantly killed by a car driven by Dominic Blum, an aqueduct racetrack officer and son of a New York police office.

I want to take a minute and talk about one of my favorite places in Queens - Howard Beach. It's basically an all-Italian community. Howard Beach was established in 1897 by William J. Howard, a Brooklyn glove manufacturer who operated a 150-acre goat farm as a source of skin for kid gloves. Is Howard Beach a good neighborhood? It is a town where everyone seemed to know everyone. There are small shops along Cross Bay Boulevard, such as bakeries, bagel shop, and a few clothing stores. People care about each other and would help others in need. Howard Beach is a neighborhood in the southwestern portion of New York City borough of Queens with a ZIP Code of 11414. Howard Beach is noted for its great Italian restaurants, like New Park Pizzeria, Bruno's Restaurant, Gino's Pizzeria, Don Pepe's, Lenny's Clam Bar and Restaurant, Russo's on the Bay, the Cross Bay diner, Prima Pasta and Café, and Divino Pizzeria & Restaurant. Take my word for it – I've been to all of these Italian restaurants, and the food is great in every single one of them. If you are ever in the area, please check out Howard Beach.

I want to talk about where it all started – Ellis Island, the island of hope. Millions and millions of immigrants came to this tiny island off of New York City from 1892 to 1954. Ellis Island was the first stop in America. It had to be. Until they passed through there, newcomers could not set foot inside the United States. Immigrants are people who leave their homeland behind, hoping for a better life. The immigrants stopping at Ellis Island mostly came from all over Europe. Many were escaping from terrible problems. Food was scarce in their homeland. There were no jobs. They were treated badly because of their religious beliefs. Although poor in money, immigrants were rich with hope. America meant freedom, jobs, and safety. "America was on everyone's lips," said one boy who came from Poland. "We talked about America. We dreamt about America. We all had one wish – to be in America.".

Ellis Island was a testing center run by the US government. Its purpose was to check immigrants and weed out the sick and unfit. The vast majority of immigrants passed the test. They were free to go ashore and start their new life. Those who failed the test were not allowed into the United States and were sent back to where they came from on ships. This earned Ellis Island its other name – the Island of Tears.

The immigrants traveled across the Atlantic Ocean, crammed into ships that generally took 7 to 10 days to reach America. After a hard day at sea, they entered New York Harbor and caught sight of two small islands - Ellis Island, of course, and Liberty island, where the Statue of Liberty holds up a flaming torch. For over 125 years, the Statue of Liberty has stood tall as a symbol of freedom in New York. The statue was a gift of friendship from the people of France to the people of the United States in 1903. A poem at the base of the statue welcomes immigrants to America. Its famous last lines are a ringing welcome from America to its immigrants. "Give me your tired, your poor, your huddled masses yearning to breathe free, the wretched refuse of your teeming shore. Send these, the homeless, tempest tossed to me. I lift my lamp beside the golden door."

After 1954, Ellis Island became a ghost town. Buildings, once grand and stately, fell into decay. Weeds and vines grew over walls. Windows were cracked. Plaster walls crumbled inside. Rain rotted the floors. Thieves snuck onto the deserted island, stealing everything from doorknobs to dishes. Ellis Island was a wreck. Then, in 1965, President Lyndon Johnson declared Ellis Island a historic site. "For nearly three decades, Ellis Island was a symbol of freedom for millions," he said. Johnson put the National Park Service in charge of the site.

I want to talk about Fiorello LaGuardia from 1882 to 1947. His Italian father was Catholic and his immigrant mother from Austria-Hungary was Jewish. Able to speak five languages, LaGuardia worked as an interpreter at Ellis Island for three years while going to law school. He was known as one of the kindest officials on the island. After law school, LaGuardia spent much of his time pleading cases for immigrants. Then politics drew him away from the law. In 1916, LaGuardia was elected to the US House of Representatives. In 1933, he became mayor of New York City. During his 12 years in office, he oversaw the building of playgrounds, parks, and low-cost housing neighborhoods. Today in New York, one of the nation's largest airports bears his name. On September 10, 1990, Ellis Island was reopened. Its purpose was to recall the human drama that occurred within its walls. Today Ellis Island National Monument is one of the most popular historic landmarks in the country. It's not surprising that the two million people who visit each year arrive by ferry, just as the immigrants did.

In November 2020, I had an emergency and had to stop writing for quite some time. Let me start from the beginning. One day I was walking my dog, Bebe, and I felt a little pain on the left side of my heart. When I stopped walking, the pain disappeared. It went on like this for two weeks. I was definitely in denial but I knew something was wrong. My inner voice told me I should go see my heart doctor, so I made an appointment. I knew I was in trouble. Dr. Sherman, my heart specialist, took an EKG, or echocardiogram, which takes about 100 pictures of your chest. The results of my EKG showed that one artery 90% blocked and the other 75%. I was in big trouble now. I had to report to Mount Sinai in Manhattan for more tests. They were unable to put in a stent, which mean I would have to go for a triple bypass. Major, major surgery. I was scared, really scared. My mind was all over the place. The first thing that came to my mind was that I wanted to take my pistol and call it a day. But then I thought, *that's the easy way out,* and I decided to go for the triple bypass. I reported to Mount Sinai hospital in Manhattan. I had to go through more tests, COVID-19 being one of them. Blood tests, EKG, and stress test all over again, and I had to answer a million questions. I was pushed into the surgical room for this major operation. I turned my life over to God. When I woke up after the operation, I had a breathing tube down my throat. I had a tube going into my penis. I had two tubes on the left side of my chest and two tubes on the right side of my chest training fluid, and I also had a port on the right side of my neck. I looked and felt like Frankenstein, and I am not kidding. It was a horrible situation. I stayed in the hospital for 11 days. It was torture - nurses shoving pills down my throat, hitting me with injections every 15 minutes, taking blood pressure nonstop. I couldn't get any sleep. The food sucked; hospital food is the worst in the world, and then I was forced to get up out of my bed, so weak and tired. They forced me to walk. I'm sure they knew what they were doing. But God, it wasn't easy. So, after 11 days of being in the hospital my nephew Frankie came to pick up his uncle. I was glad I was going home, but I was also afraid of being alone and dying in my apartment. In the hospital, I was safe. Nurses and doctors were there in case something should happen. When my nephew dropped me off, I felt strange being home. I was weak and disoriented and couldn't focus. My wife, Theresa, was there to greet me. It was nice to see her, but I didn't want her to see me in this weak condition. Now I was home alone. Fear took over my entire being. There were no nurses, no doctors to check up on me, but it was something I had to deal with. Thank God my apartment is small and it was easy getting around from room to room. Going to bed produced the worst excruciating pain and I couldn't sleep. My mind was exhausted. I had bad thoughts of committing suicide but I said to myself, that's the easy way out. So as time went on, I started to adjust to this new way of life, praying to God to give me strength to carry on. The pain was so bad, I was taking a painkiller by the name of Oxy like candy. I had no choice. Oxycodone can be very habit-forming. But I slept like a baby. Thank God for Oxy. I was told by the visiting nurse that I had to get up and move around. He was afraid that pneumonia might set in – yes, water in my lungs. I would be finished, so I had to get my ass up from bed and move around, which I did. Besides having a physical problem, I also had a mental problem - depression. I had thoughts of being rushed back to the hospital, cutting open my chest again, stopping my heart. I couldn't handle going through this all over again. I only had negative thoughts. It took some time at home to realize that I was alive and God decided not to take me and that he would give me a few more years on this earth for reasons I don't know. I had my surgery November 5, 2020 it is now January 5, 2021. It's been eight weeks that I've been home and I still don't feel a hundred percent. I was told by the surgeon it will take anywhere from three to six months to get back to normal. To me, that seems like a long time. I have a visiting nurse that comes twice a week to see if I'm dead or alive. He checks my blood pressure, the rate of my heart, and has me walk around the apartment. The visiting nurse also checks that I'm taking the right medication. I'm hoping by the month of June, I could go on a long cruise. I'm looking forward to hopping on the Royal Caribbean going out of Bayonne, New Jersey. I can't wait. I need this vacation. I want to thank all the nurses at Mount Sinai Hospital and the surgeon, especially, for saving my life.

I can't believe it is now January 2021. *God, where do the years go?* That was always something I said, even when I was young. I wish I could stop the clock but I know that's not going to happen. Anyway, I'm still recovering from my open-heart surgery, but, all in all, I'm doing okay. I am a little disappointed this year. Donald Trump was not reelected; I know a lot of you are happy about that. But this is what democracy is all about - the people make the final decision. I was a Democrat all my life until Donald Trump came down the escalator with his wife. What really drew me to Donald Trump was that he was an outsider and not a politician, and I felt in my heart that he loves this country and is very patriotic. He was for the people, he spoke his mind and wasn't afraid to do so. And the idea of building a wall to stop all those from coming into this country was a great idea because it would stop disease, crime, rape from coming into this country. We have enough problems in this country. God help us without bringing people in from all over the world. We need to wake up. We have people living in cardboard boxes. People are starving. They have no food to eat. There are no jobs, and politicians keep ripping us off. They are not for the people. The rich get richer and the poor get poorer. Governor Cuomo is giving driving licenses to illegal immigrants. What is happening to this country do you know why Governor Cuomo is giving licenses to illegal immigrants? I'll tell you why. It's all about the money, God help us. For years, the Democrats tried everything in their power to take this president down and nothing worked. They even went after his family. Nancy Pelosi is an evil bitch and has no compassion for the poor people in this country, except showing off her refrigerator with all her expensive ice cream while people are starving in the streets. 75 million people voted for Trump and now the Democrats are saying those 75 million people need to be deprogrammed. This is not the Democratic Party that I belonged to of JFK.

In my opinion, the government is supposed to make life easier for its citizens. JFK was a great president. JFK had a great phrase. *Ask not what your country can do for you, ask what you can do for your country.* I wonder what would have happened if JFK had been able to win a second term as president. The next election for the president was going to be in 1964. By late 1963, he was already thinking about his campaign. He decided to travel to Texas, the home state of vice president Lyndon Johnson. Many people close to JFK worried about the trip to Texas. The crowds in Texas might be unfriendly. By lunchtime, thousands of people had gathered to see the Kennedys pass by. A moment later, shots rang out. Someone in the limousine shouted out, "No, no, no, the president has been hit." JFK slumped over to his wife Jackie. Her pink suit was splattered with blood. The car sped through the streets to the nearest hospital, but it was too late. Doctors confirmed the awful news. John Fitzgerald Kennedy was dead. I had two major tragedies in my lifetime. The assassination of John F. Kennedy and the bombing of the World Trade Center in 2001.

I want to talk about another person that I admired in my lifetime growing up. His name was Walt Disney. Born on December 5 1901, in his early years, Walt Disney actually worked for the United States Postal Service. What I really remember about growing up with Walt Disney was a cartoon character that he came up with - the one and only Mickey Mouse! The kids went absolutely crazy and let's not forget the Mickey Mouse Club, which was a big hit. I remember all the kids became club members all over the world. It was a great time for animated cartoons. In my opinion, Walt Disney was a genius. Walt Disney was always looking for the next big idea. He created Snow White and the Seven Dwarfs. It took many years to create. It took more than three years to make Snow White Times Magazine calls Snow White a masterpiece. Walt Disney created so many cartoon characters, including Donald Duck, Mickey Mouse, Minnie Mouse, Pinocchio, Bambi, Peter Pan, Alice in Wonderland, Sleeping Beauty ... I could go on and on. Until 1964, people did not know that smoking causes cancer. Walt became extremely sick, having been a chain smoker all his life. The results came back and the doctors told him he had lung cancer. Walt Disney was 65 years old. He did not live to see the opening of Walt Disney World in Florida in 1971.

It is now February 2, 2021 and I want to talk about life in general and the mistakes we all make. It is a subtle reminder that everything - the good and bad, pleasure and pain, approval and disapproval, achievements and mistakes, fame and shame - all come and go. Everything has a beginning and an ending. And that's the way it's supposed to be. Every experience we have ever had ends. Every thought you have had started and finished. Every emotion and mood you've experienced has been replaced by another. You've been happy, sad, jealous, depressed, angry, shamed, proud, and every other conceivable human feeling. When did they all go? The answer is, no one really knows. All we really know is that eventually, everything disappears into nothingness. Welcoming this truth into your life is the beginning of liberating adventure. Our disappointment comes about in essentially two ways. When we're experiencing pleasure, we want it to last forever. It never does. When we are experiencing pain, we want it to go away now. It usually doesn't. Unhappiness is a result of struggling against the natural flow of experience. It's enormously helpful to experiment with the awareness that life is just one thing after another. One present moment followed by another present moment. When something is happening that we enjoy, know that while it's wonderful to experience the happiness it brings, it will eventually be replaced by something else. If that's okay with you, you'll feel peace even when the moment changes. And if you're experiencing some type of pain or displeasure, know that this too shall pass. Keeping this awareness close to your heart is a wonderful way to maintain your perspective, even in the face of adversity. It's not always easy, but it is usually helpful. Live this day as if it were your last. It might be. When are you going to die? In 50 years, 20 years, 10, 5, today? Last time I checked, no one had told me. I often wonder, when listening to the news, did the person who died in the auto accident on his way home from work remember to tell his family how much he loved them? The truth is, none of us has any idea how long we have. Sadly, however, we act as if we're going to live forever. We postpone the things that, deep down, we know we want to do - telling the people we love how much we care. But to remind you of how precious life really is, a friend of mine once said, "life is too important to take too seriously." Ten years later, I knew he was right.

If I can, I want to talk about how humility and peace go hand in hand. The less compelled you are to prove yourself to others, the easier it is to feel peaceful inside. Proving yourself is a dangerous trap, it takes an enormous amount of energy to be continually proving your accomplishments, bragging, or trying to convince others of your worth as a human being. Bragging actually dilutes the positive feelings you receive from an accomplishment or something you are proud of. The more you try to prove yourself, the more others will avoid you, talk behind your back about your insecurity to brag, and perhaps even resent you. Ironically, however, the less you care about seeking approval, the more approval you seem to get. People are drawn to those with a quiet, inner confidence, people who don't need to make themselves look good, be right all the time, or steal the glory. Love a person who doesn't need to brag, a person who shares from his or her heart and not from his or her ego.

Okay, let's get back to talking about growing up Italian. I wanted to talk about one of my favorite movies of all time, *Goodfellas*. There is a scene in the *Goodfellas* that I love. Ray Liotta is driving, riding shotgun is Robert DeNiro, who looks as if he's napping, and in the backseat, very still, sits Joe Pesci. It's clear from this stance that these men are, if not brothers, part of a crew and are comfortable together. A loud banging from the back of the trunk alerts them all. "What the fuck is that?" Liotta says. The car pulls over, the three men get out of the car and line up, looking at the trunk. Pesci reaches into his sports jacket, and we presume he's going to pull out a gun. Instead, he takes out a terrifyingly long and sharp, butcher knife. Liotta approaches the rear of the car, keys in hand. Inside lays a man wrapped in a sheet with blood all over his face, rasping. Pesci approaches, knife ready to strike, furious that the man is still alive, the fucking piece of shit, as he stabs through the sheet several times. DeNiro, whose face had an expression one could read as disapproving, steps up, revolver in hand, and fires four bullets into the body. When *Goodfellas* first hit the theaters in 1990, a classic was born. It had unparalleled influence on pop-culture, one that would inspire future filmmakers and redefine the gangster picture as we know it today. Goodfellas is frequently cited as the most realistic American movie about organized crime ever made, from the rush of grotesque violence in the opening scene to the iconic hilarity of Joe Pesci's endlessly quoted, "Funny how? Funny like a clown?" *Goodfellas* is a great movie about organized crime because, among other things, it constantly pushes beyond ordinary realism. Goodfellas, indeed, is based on a true story. Remember, there are five families in New York City. Besides *Goodfellas,* there's another mob movie called *Casino* with Robert DeNiro. One of my favorite all-time movies, *Casino* is one of the greatest movies about Las Vegas, directed by Martin Scorsese. This iconic movie, released in 1995, tells the story of two mobsters who are best friends and try to create their own casino empire. The most exciting thing is that the plot is based on the true story of Frank Lefty Rosenthal, played by Robert De Niro, and his real-life gangster friend, Tony Spilotro, played by Joe Pesci. Before filming *Casino,* Robert De Niro met the man on whom his character Sam Rothstein is based. He met with Frank Rosenthal in person. Not many people know that the Tangier's casino didn't really exist. Tangiers's casino was just a fiction, but the film was shot in a real operating casino called the Riviera. Aside from DeNiro and Pesci, the movie starred Sharon Stone as Ginger Mckenna, James Woods as Lester Diamond, Don Rickles as Billy Sherbet and Alan King as Andy Stone. Another one of my favorite movies is *A Bronx Tale,* a 1993 American crime drama film directed by Robert DeNiro, his directional debut, and produced by Jane Rosenthal, adapted from Chazz Palminteri's 1989 play of the same name. It tells the coming-of-age story of an Italian American boy, Calogero, who, after encountering a local Mafia boss, is torn between the temptations of organized crime, racism in his community, and the values of his honest, hard-working father. The Broadway production was converted to film with limited changes and starred DeNiro. DeNiro, who first viewed the play in Los Angeles in 1990, acquired the rights from Palminteri, intent on making the play his directional debut. The duo worked heavily together on the screenplay, with Palminteri aiming to retain many of the aspects of the original script, as it was based largely on his own childhood. Production began in 1991 and was funded in collaboration with DeNiro's Tribeca Productions and Savoy Pictures, the first film released by each studio. A Bronx Tale premiered at the Toronto International Film Festival on September 14, 1993, and was released in the United States on September 29, 1993. The film achieved limited commercial success, grossing over 17 million domestically. However, it fared much better with critics, who praised the performances of the leads, and launched Palminteri's acting career, while also helping DeNiro gain acceptance as a director.

I have an interesting subject I want to talk about - superstitions in Italy, which are largely themed around death. I'm going to give you a list of the craziness

1. The Broom. Single people, don't let a broom touch your feet when someone is cleaning the floors. If you do, you will never be swept off your feet and get married.
   2. The Black Cat. Most Italians would give pause, and a truly superstitious one might throw a hissy fit, before they would cross paths with one. On the other hand, it's considered a good bit of feline fortune. If you happen to hear a cat sneeze.
2. The Hat. When the sick are close to death, a priest comes to receive their final confessions. The priest will remove his hat and set it on the bed so that he could put on the vestments. Thus, a hat's temporary resting place is associated with eternal rest, a thought that keeps Italians from sleeping peacefully.
3. The Number 13. The number 13 is considered lucky in Italy. Associated with the great goddess, fertility and the lunar cycles, the number is thought to bring prosperity and life, quite the opposite view than that of the Western world.
4. Spilling olive oil. Most likely due to the fact that it was historically such an expensive commodity, spilling olive oil is believed to bring bad luck in Italy. If you do happen to make a blunder, dab some of the spilled oil behind each ear to rectify your mistake.
5. When making a toast in Italy, it's considered unlucky to do so with water. So do as the locals and make your toast with wine.

Have you ever heard someone say, don't step on a crack, you'll break your mother's back? Or, find a penny, pick it up and all day long, you'll have good luck? These sayings are among many that represent one's intention of adding protection against bad luck. The blessing or exorcism of a new house in Italy is still practiced, especially when it comes to newlyweds. Moving into a first home was accompanied by the necessary rituals to rid the place of any spirits that may have been left by the previous owners and could harm the new couple, or their first child. A new broom is a common first gift to sweep away evil spirits. Sprinkled salt in the corners of the house will purify it. The neighborhood priest goes house to house before Easter to bless each home with holy water.

One thing I have to say about growing up Italian in Brooklyn is that my family didn't have a lot of money, but we always had food in the refrigerator. Today we have a million gadgets - air fryers, fast cookers, slow cookers. My grandmother had one frying pan and she cooked everything in that one pan. Today these young people have all these gadgets and they still can't cook a decent meal. Oh, I forgot - most of the young people don't cook at all. Fast food is their thing. This is why they all have stomach problems and obesity is common with young people. No exercise, sitting watching TV on the couch, stuffing their face with potato chips and pretzels. I mean I never heard of a 13-year-old having high blood pressure. It's got to be from all the shit they eat. Okay, enough about putting down the young people.

I want to talk about the history of Campania Italy, where my parents came from. I have been researching the history of Campania about a year ago, when I started writing this book. My mother was from Naples. I have traced my grandmother's family back centuries. I have never been there but hope one day before I drop dead that I will go. Campania is cheerful and radiant, well known for the typical products from the land. Thanks to the sun, this region can boast the juiciest and tastiest tomatoes in the world. I would say that the most popular dish in Naples is their famous thin crust pizza which, by the way, is my favorite. Another famous food of Naples is spaghetti with white clam sauce. Another one of my favorite all-time dishes is the caprese salad, and I've got to mention Buffalo mozzarella is out of this world. All you need is a loaf of Italian bread and the deal is done. And for dessert, let's not forget *sfogliatelle*. Mama mia, that goes great with a nice cappuccino.

To change the subject a little, as I'm getting up in age, comes the opportunity for listening. Indeed, sometimes listening is forced upon us, as an old friend said one day, after long years spent in acquiring experience, "I find now that no one is interested in my wisdom." Once you retire from the mainstream of daily activity, no one expects your views to make that much sense anymore. Once you come to age, you find that the world gives you a lot more time to listen. The experience is not all bad. It can be a relief to sit back and no longer be expected to make sensible statements. For the first time in your life, you have the opportunity to analyze the absurdity of others, the time to appreciate the innocent wisdom of children, the chance to listen. And hear what friends are not saying to perceive the deepest feelings quietly revealed by their inattention by going to your retirement party and suddenly finding oneself on the outside of the circle busily centered on someone else who speaks to them of the future rather than the past. Listening may be the last best activity of a long life. I find now that I'm up in age. Young people don't have the patience to listen to us. We take too long with our words, and sometimes we repeat ourselves. One day, it will happen to them and then they will understand.

Okay. I'm back. It's been a couple of months. I couldn't think of anything to put on paper. That's why it's called writers block. It's a condition primarily associated with writing, in which an author is unable to produce new work or experiences a creative slowdown. The creative goal is not the result of commitment problems or the lack of writing skills.

President Biden, the worst president in my lifetime, became president in 2020. The United States of America is being totally destroyed. They say 80 million people voted for this moron.

I want to talk a little bit about Afghanistan. Thousands of American citizens and our allies were left behind enemy lines to be slaughtered, and this president turns his back on the American people. What a disgrace. I know this book is about growing up Italian but I can't keep it inside. The disgust I feel over what is happening to this beautiful country of ours. This president of ours can't even complete a sentence. He mumbles and fumbles over and over again. It's an embarrassment to the American people. He has only been in office for 12 months. God help us for the next three years. When Donald Trump was president, I was paying two dollars a gallon for gas. You know what I'm paying for gas now? A little over four dollars a gallon and its going higher. This moron of a president is begging foreign countries for gas and oil again. When Donald Trump was president, we were energy independent.

I could go on and on and I'm going to. Let's talk about the southern border aliens - and I called them aliens - from all over the world coming into this country with all kinds of diseases, including the virus. No one coming into the country is being tested. The

Democratic Party in my opinion is anti-American. This is not the Democratic Party of my parents. This is why when I saw Donald Trump coming down the escalator, I crossed over to the Republican Party. Its's the best thing I ever did. Going back to the aliens coming into this country. Our young people are dying by the thousands from drug overdoses being brought in across the border from the cartels, the White House and the president of the United States. They don't give a shit. The 80 million people voted for Biden should be very happy. What's going on in this country? You deserve everything you get and more. Don't worry, more disgrace is coming to this country as long as this president is in office. The Vice President Kamala Harris is another one who hasn't done shit for this country. President Biden put her in charge of the border. What a disaster. She has no idea what the hell's going on in this country when she can't answer a question. She giggles like a moron. It's such an embarrassment, it hurts me to see this country being destroyed by anti-Americans. The vice president's salary is 230,700 a year. Not a bad salary for doing nothing.

I want to go back to the disaster in Afghanistan, where thousands of American citizens are being slaughtered. The women are being raped. Thanks to President Biden for turning his back on the American people. I wonder if his family was behind enemy lines in Afghanistan would he turned his back on them. I know one thing for sure, if Trump was in office now, none of this would be happening. Putin, the dictator of Russia, was deadly afraid of President Trump. How is it possible that one person can destroy the whole entire country? I'm hoping and praying that in November 2022, the Republicans take the house. I believe people in this country. It's only been 12 months since Biden became president and the American people are tired of the bullshit. The Biden administration is being backed up by the FBI and the CIA and the media. It's all corruption. I will never forget what President Biden did in Afghanistan. The Taliban had taken hold about 20 or 30% of the country. Biden had his finger up his ass and did nothing, but by the time he woke up from his nap, it was too late. There were thousands of American citizens trapped behind enemy lines and thousands of our allies also trapped. Did Biden give a fuck? No, he was thinking about his favorite flavor of ice cream, turning his back on the American people. Shameful.

Let me continue about the weakness this president shows he gets up to make a speech and his eyes are closing. Most likely he forgot to take his nap. God help us. Pres. Biden's famous saying is, *Come on, man* ... I remember him saying that he was going to take Donald Trump in the back of the schoolyard and beat the shit out of him. Really Joe. I'm getting sleepy now it's 3 o'clock in the morning. It is time for my nap time. Come back, Joe. I mean this from the bottom of my heart. I want you to succeed for the good of this country. But I know deep in my heart it's not going to happen. I have bad news for you, Joe. The Republicans will take the house in November 2022. You can take that to the bank.

Now let me talk about the vice president Kamala Harris, who is a complete moron and has no idea what the hell is going on in this country. You have the blind leading the blind. God help us. I don't have to tell you how she got up there climbing the ladder. I'll leave that up to your own imagination. Writing about these morons is making my pressure go up. If this president doesn't step down, World War III is upon us. I don't understand how one person can destroy the United States. It's a disgrace in plain English. Inflation is killing the American people, prices are going through the roof. People can't afford to drive their cars at the pump. What the hell is going on? I'll tell you what is going on. The rich are getting richer and the poor are getting poorer. I don't understand, we give billions to foreign countries and yet we have people in our own country living in cardboard boxes. The country of Ukraine is being completely demolished and the Russian president is calling the shots. Civilians, women and children are being slaughtered by the thousands and the United States is the strongest military in the world and we are just sitting back and watching these innocent people being slaughtered. What a shame. President Biden wants open borders. People from all over the world, including Africa coming into this country, not being tested for the virus, putting Americans in harm's way, bringing all kinds of diseases, not only Covid but HIV, syphilis, gonorrhea, herpes, and I could go on and on.

Okay, let's go back to growing up Italian. This picture is from the Bronx Tale. One of my favorite movies. Robert De Niro played a great part in this movie as a bus driver. The guy with the stick ball bat also played a great part. His name is Chazz Palminteri.

Growing up at 587 Grand Street in Brooklyn, NY brings back so many good memories. My sisters and I had such good times. We had two great parents who gave us what little they had. I think about them all the time. They are always in my heart. My mother always had a smile even in the darkest days. I get tears in my eyes just thinking about her. Such a good soul. Everyone loved Dora. My mother was 5'7" tall and always well-dressed with jet black hair. When my mother got angry or mad, she would always bite her finger. I would get hit on the head with a wooden spoon or shoes thrown at the back of my head.

When you go to a restaurant today, they always serve you the salad first. In an Italian family, the salad is always served last why? For digestion. It's now 2 o'clock in the morning and am getting sleepy and saying my prayers. Hoping I get up in the morning to continue.

Okay I'm back now. I had writers block for a few months where I couldn't think of anything to say. There is so much going on in this world. It's such a big distraction. Ever since President Biden got into office, everything seems to be upside down. Let me get back to my family and not to be distracted by a President who is incompetent to run this country. I remember when I was little growing up in Brooklyn, we would make box scooters. It was a wooden box connected by a 2 x 4 with roller skates in the front and back of the 2 x 4. We used the wheels from the roller skates. It was more like competition for who made their own box scooters. We had lots of fun back in the days. There's one very important lesson I learned in my lifetime and that is you can't go back.

I will never forget the measles. In the 1950s me and my two sisters almost died from that devastating disease, and not long after that another devastating disease - the chickenpox. It turned out to be a bad virus, killing more than 142,000 people. So where did the measles and the chickenpox come from Africa. That's right, Africa. Crazy people doing experiments on animals and also having sex with animals, it's disgusting - bats, monkeys, and who knows what else. The world we are living in today is upside down. You know, to live your life the way you choose, you have to be a bit rebellious. You have to be willing to stand up for yourself. You might have to be a bit disturbing to those who have a strong interest in controlling your behavior, but if you're willing, you'll find that being your own person, not letting others do your thinking for you, is a joyful, worldly, and absolutely silly way to live. You need not be a revolutionary, just a human being who says to the world, and everyone in it, I am going to be my own person, and resist anyone who tries to stop me. A well-known popular song tells us life is a beautiful thing. As *long as I hold the string, I'll be a silly so-and-so... If I should ever let it go ...* You don't want to be manipulated by other people pulling the strings. Many people are more content to be regulated to take charge of their own lives. If you don't mind having your strings being pulled, that's on you. You must remember no one else can live your life, feel what you feel, get into your body to experience the world the way you do. This is the only life you get. It is only logical that you should determine how you are going to function, and your functioning ought to bring the joy and fulfillment of pulling your own strings. No one else can live your life. Feel what you feel. Get into your body and experience the world the way you do. This is the only life you get. It is too precious to let others take their own advantage of it. Perhaps the best way to achieve freedom in your life is to remember this guideline: never place total reliance in anyone other than yourself when it comes to guiding your life. Nothing in this world can bring you peace but yourself. Courage means flying in the face of criticism, relying on yourself, being willing to accept and learn from the consequences of all your choices. So that you can cut the strings whose ends other people hold and use to pull you in a contrary direction. You can make your mental leaps toward courage by repeatedly asking yourself, what is the worst thing that could happen to me if.... When you consider the possibilities realistically, you will always find that nothing damaging or painful can happen when you take the necessary steps away from being a knee-jerk victim. Usually you will find that, like a child afraid of the dark, you are afraid of nothing, because nothing is the worst thing that could happen to you. We are all victims and need to stand up for ourselves.

As much as some people try to deny it, no one gets off this planet alive. Life in fact is a terminal disease. I want to talk about becoming very destructive toward your own body. Yours is the only body you will ever get, so why make it something that isn't healthy, attractive, and wonderful to be around. By letting yourself get fat through improper diet and lack of exercise, you victimize yourself. By not giving your body adequate rest periods or by fouling it up with stress and tension, you are allowing yourself to be victimized. Your body is a powerful, well-tuned, highly efficient instrument, but you can abuse it in so many ways by simply rejecting it, or fueling it with low caliber fuels and addictive substances that will only diminish it in the end.

In the month of May 2023, I went to the doctor for a checkup. He checked my heart and did an ultrasound of the carotid artery in my neck. To my surprise, he seemed a little worried and told me the left side of my neck was okay. The right side of my neck is another story. I had a blockage of 70%. Not good. He told me to make an appointment with a surgeon in Mount Sinai Hospital in Manhattan, which I did. If I decided not to go for surgery, I would definitely have a stroke. So after open-heart surgery in 2020, I went back again to Mount Sinai to do carotid artery surgery on my neck. It's a very dangerous operation because the piece of plaque from the carotid artery can break off and go to the brain. You could have a stroke. The surgeon decided to put a stent in the carotid artery to keep it open, so more blood flow would go to the brain. Surgery was scheduled for May 16, 2023, and I had to be there at six in the morning. That was a Tuesday. I stayed one night and I was discharged on Wednesday. It's good to be home. Now it's a matter of taking it easy, recuperating one day at a time.

I just want to say it's been a long journey writing this book, which is generally about family and the way I grew up in Brooklyn, remembering the good times and bad times. I have great memories and bad memories, but I guess that's what life is all about. I want to end this book by telling my son Jason to always be true to himself. Don't let anyone change your mind. If you truly believe it's right, you only have one life to live, live it like it's your last, years go by very quickly. Always try to do the right thing and never make the same mistake. Never be afraid to say what's on your mind. If the weight of life is pulling you down, look up, look around and He will always be there for you. Pray and go to church because life is hard knocks. Be strong and never give up. Love you always - DAD.